Leader's Guide

Guided Meditations on Images of God

Leader's Guide

Guided Meditations on Images of God: Mother, Potter, Compassion, Love

Jane E. Ayer

Saint Mary's Press
Christian Brothers Publications
Winona, Minnesota

Genuine recycled paper with 10% post-consumer waste.
Printed with soy-based ink.

The publishing team for this book included Carl Koch, development editor;
Rebecca Fairbank, copy editor; James H. Gurley, production editor; Cindi
Ramm, cover designer; SuperStock, cover photo; pre-press, printing, and
binding by the graphics division of Saint Mary's Press.

The acknowledgments continue on page 46.

Printed in the United States of America

Printing: 9 8 7 6 5 4 3 2 1

Year: 2007 06 05 04 03 02 01 00 99

ISBN 0-88489-609-9

Contents

Directions for Leading the Meditations   7

Mother: I Will Never Forget You   12

Potter: Shaped and Reshaped   21

Compassion: In the Belly
         of the Great Fish   29

Love: Reflection in the Mirror   37

To Pauline,
with a grateful heart
for the image of a gentle, loving God
grown in tender, fertile friendship

Directions
for Leading the Meditations

LEADER PREPARATION As the meditation leader, your preparation is especially important to the success of a guided meditation. Pray the meditation before leading a group in it. This will help you to become comfortable with its style and content. Some materials may require a brief doctrinal review with the group. By praying the meditation first, you will become aware if there is a need to do this.

If you choose to have your group do an optional art expression as a follow-up to the meditations, it is best if you try it out before the group gathers to make sure it works well and to know better what directions to give.

If you intend to guide the meditations yourself rather than use the accompanying cassette or compact disc, rehearse the guided prayer, including the introductory comments, the scriptural reading, and the opening and closing prayers, so that appropriate and sufficient time is allowed for the imagery to take place and for prayerful reflection to occur. The meditations should be read slowly and prayerfully, using soft instrumental music as a background.

Only a good reader who has prepared should read aloud the scriptural passage that precedes each guided meditation. The scriptural passage is important to establishing the theme and the tone of the meditation. Read it with reverence and expression, using a Bible.

PARTICIPANT PREPARATION To introduce praying a guided meditation, it might be helpful to explain that the participants will be using a prayer form that will call upon their imagination, and that the Holy Spirit graces our imagination during prayer to help us communicate with God. Remember that this type of prayer may not be easy for everyone in the group. Some may be self-conscious about closing their eyes; some may have difficulty getting in touch with their feelings; some may have personal obstacles in their relationship with God. Sometimes it helps to reassure the participants that if they cannot "get into it," they can use the quiet time to just slow themselves down, relax, and talk to the Lord in their own way. The participants can also be told that although the meditation is guided, if the Spirit leads them in another direction, it is okay for them to go with their own reflection and not worry about the words being spoken. Be gentle, let go, and let the Spirit work.

A possible difficulty, one that may not be apparent at first, may be encountered by those who wear the type of contact lenses that prevent them from closing their eyes for an extended period of time. Invite these participants to put their head down, hiding their eyes in the dark crook of their arm, if they are unable to remove the lenses. Another possible difficulty may be experienced by those who have a sinus problem or asthma. Instead of breathing through their nose during the deep-breathing exercises, they can breathe quietly through their mouth. Also, during the relaxation and centering phases of the meditation, the span of time for holding the breath should be very brief.

MUSIC Quiet instrumental music is important for setting and keeping the mood of the meditation. Music can be playing even as the group gathers. It is a nice background for giving instructions. Have additional tapes or compact discs ready to play during the activities after the guided meditation. Ideally, the follow-up activities will take place in a separate space; therefore, it is less disruptive if cassette or CD players are already set up in the different areas.

REFLECTION QUESTIONS Allowing time for the participants to reflect and name the experiences they have just gone through is a necessary part of these prayer experiences. The reflection questions will help the participants do this successfully. Choose several reflection questions (or use questions similar to them) and type them up, leaving room after each for a response. Make a copy for each participant. Allow enough time for each person to respond to the questions and to share his or her responses with the group. These prayer experiences are not meant to be rushed.

To avoid disrupting the quiet mood of the meditation time, pass out the reflection questions (facedown) as the participants take their places. Also, give a pen or pencil to each person. If people are sitting on the floor, you could pass out hardcover books or clipboards to facilitate writing. Explain that you are distributing reflection questions for use after the meditation.

Assure the participants that their responses are private and that their papers are not going to be collected. When it is time for sharing, honor and affirm all responses, and respect those persons who do not wish to answer aloud.

ART EXPRESSION AND PRAYER RITUAL (OPTIONAL)

Each prayer experience comes with optional art expressions, each containing a prayer ritual. You might choose to use an art expression rather than the reflection questions because the participants tend to share more readily with something meaningful and tangible in their hands.

If you choose to do an optional art expression, prepare the art materials ahead of time and lay them out in the area where the participants will work. Familiarize the group with the art activity before the prayer time, if possible, so as not to disrupt the meditative mood. This should allow you to give particular directions for the art activity without having to answer a lot of questions. If you have previously completed the art expression, it might be helpful to show your sample artwork at this time.

SETTING

It is imperative that the area for the prayer experience is quiet—no ringing of telephones, bells, and the like. If necessary, put a sign on the outside of your door: Praying! Please do not disturb!

Participants may sit in chairs or find a comfortable position on the floor, but they must be a few feet from one another so that they each have their own space and do not distract one another. Therefore, the area must be large enough so the participants are not cramped. Lying down on the floor should be discouraged, as some participants are likely to fall asleep.

CENTERPIECE (OPTIONAL)

Each theme of the prayer experiences can be enhanced by creating a centerpiece that can be placed on a small table, an altar, or the middle of the floor. The centerpiece should include candles, a Bible opened to the scriptural passage, and objects that reflect the message of the prayer. For example, for the meditation on God as mother ("I Will Never Forget You"), you might display a baby blanket, a small pillow, a cradle or doll's bed, toys, stuffed animals—all decoratively arranged on a pastel cloth.

A centerpiece for the meditation on God as potter ("Shaped and Reshaped") might include whole, broken, and chipped pieces of pottery; and a block of clay—all displayed on a mustard yellow or light green cloth.

To enhance the meditation on God as compassion ("In the Belly of the Great Fish"), the centerpiece might consist of photos or magazine cutouts of persons of various cultures and ages surrounding a stuffed toy whale or a picture of a whale, or a picture of Jonah and the whale—all positioned on a light blue cloth.

To set the theme for the meditation on God as love ("Reflection in the Mirror"), the centerpiece might display heart-shaped boxes, containers, or cutouts; various mirrors; and red or pink candles—all arranged attractively on a red, pink, or white cloth.

MATERIALS NEEDED

- a Bible
- an audiotape or CD player
- the meditation recording or script
- tapes or CDs of instrumental music

- reflection questions (a copy for each participant)
- pens or pencils
- clipboards or hardcover books to facilitate writing, if needed
- materials for the art expression (optional; see individual project's needs)
- a centerpiece to reflect the theme (optional)
- a sign that reads Praying! Please do not disturb!

Mother
I Will Never Forget You

This reflective prayer experience, "I Will Never Forget You," is based on Isaiah's passage in which God is imaged with a maternal love. It reminds us of the faithful and nurturing tenderness with which God holds us. God's love will never fail, even if other loves do.

THEME   After you have given directions to the participants and set the tone for meditation, introduce the theme by saying something like the following:

> Imaging our God as a mother opens the potential for a deeply felt love. Trusting that we are held with gentle care allows for the healing of wounds and the growth of our own capacity to nurture. We can experience the tenderness of our Mother God if we allow ourselves to risk and be cuddled in our quiet place apart.

OPENING   Read aloud this opening prayer:

> Mother God, you are the God who loves us. . . . Us!
> . . . born of your heart and womb, yet beneath the beating of another's heart and from another's womb. Grant us these moments of relating to you as mother so that we might come to know more fully your deep and faithful love for us. We ask this petition from the source of your tender love. Amen.

SCRIPTURE   Read aloud Isaiah 49:14–15, using a Bible.

SCRIPT Play the "I Will Never Forget You" meditation on the accompanying recording, or slowly and reverently read aloud the following script for the guided meditation. Play soft, instrumental background music.

> Today you will enter the hush of your quiet place in your imagination and meet Mary, who will help you to experience God as mother. First, you will begin by doing some deep-breathing exercises. When I say to, if you can, breathe in and out through your nose very quietly during these exercises. Close your eyes and get comfortable. You will be relaxing your entire body.
>
> Breathe in deeply . . . hold it . . . breathe out slowly and completely. Breathe in deeply . . . hold it . . . breathe out slowly and completely. Again, breathe in deeply . . . hold it . . . breathe out slowly and completely.
>
> Allow your feet and ankles to relax. . . . Relax your legs . . . and your hips. . . . Stay mindful of your breathing. Relax your stomach muscles . . . and now your chest. . . . Just relax. . . . Let your arms grow limp. . . . Relax your wrists, . . . your hands, . . . and your fingers. . . . Keep breathing in deeply and out slowly.
>
> Allow your shoulders to become heavy. . . . Let all the tension drain from your shoulders. . . . Relax your neck, . . . your facial muscles, . . . your forehead, . . . and even your eyelids. . . . Just relax. . . . Breathe in deeply . . . hold it . . . breathe out slowly and completely. [Pause.]
>
> You are standing on soft carpeting in a pleasantly scented hallway with subdued lighting. . . .

You are facing a closed door with the word *welcome* stenciled on it. You sense there is something special in the room beyond. Go ahead . . . open the door and enter. You have stepped into a nursery. . . . Sounds of a lullaby fill the room. . . . A rocking chair sits in a corner next to the crib. . . . A recliner piled with stuffed animals fills another corner. . . . It is obvious that the room is being prepared for someone new. It is not finished yet. Take this time to complete the room and create a space that you would consider warm and inviting. [Pause.]

Sit quietly in either the rocker or recliner. . . . Think of women you've known in your life who have been loving and nurturing to you. . . . What do you feel that you gained from their loving of you? [Pause.]

Think both of women whom you know or may not personally know, but whom you have witnessed as being loving and nurturing to others . . . perhaps you saw them offering something that you yourself longed for. . . . What is it that they offered someone else that you wish you had received? [Pause.]

Now name one good quality portrayed by your own mother or someone you consider as close as a mother. [Pause.]

A rustling at the door causes you to look up. . . . Mary, the blessed mother, stands at the door. She is smiling at you with love. She greets you by name. . . . Notice how you are feeling to have Mary as company. . . .

Invite her in. . . . Mary enters and looks around; she notices what you have done to complete the nursery. Hear her comments to you about the room. [Pause.]

Mary sits and leans toward you intently. . . . She asks you, "What do you need in the way of mothering or nurturing right now in your life?" . . . Hear her say, "Trust. . . . Tell me. . . ."

Allow yourself to feel safe with Mary and share with her the empty spaces of your life. [Pause.]

With gentleness and compassion, she tells you that God loves you like, and yet more than, the tenderest woman of your memory . . . that God has held you in a way that no one else can, from the very beginning of time . . . and that God, who formed you, yearns to be the nourisher of your life . . . now and always. . . .

Listen as Mary asks you to name moments when you were aware of God's mothering in your life. [Pause.]

She reminds you that what you have known is a constant, . . . and that God is always ready to offer God's continued warmth and mothering. . . . Mary encourages you. . . . "Close your eyes. . . . Be still now . . . be still. . . ."

Invite yourself to feel the presence of a tender, loving, mothering God. . . . Allow yourself to really hear these words of your Mother God. "Would a mother forget the baby at her breast? . . . Would she forget the child in her womb? . . . Even if she forgets, I will never forget you. . . . I will never forget you, whom I have made from my own desire . . . from my own design . . . in my own image. . . . You are mine."

Allow these words to penetrate further with warmth and healing, "You are precious in my sight and I love you. . . ."

Mary reaches over and touches you. She assures you with such certitude, "You are precious in God's sight, and God does love you. . . ."

Hear Mary say, "I will leave you now to bask in the warmth of your God's mothering. . . ." Very simply she leans down and kisses you on the top of your head. She tells you now, "Image yourself in the embrace of your God. . . ." As you close your eyes, you are aware that Mary leaves the room. Hear her words again. . . . Image yourself in the embrace of your God. . . . [Pause.] Notice what you are feeling at this moment. . . .

Remain in the nursery for a few quiet moments, walk around, touch the softness of things, and most importantly, remember that you have been born from the womb and heart of a God who will never forget you. . . .

Breathe in deeply . . . hold it . . . breathe out slowly and completely. Breathe in deeply . . . hold it . . . breathe out slowly and completely. Once more, breathe in deeply . . . hold it . . . breathe out slowly and completely. And when you are ready, you may open your eyes.

REFLECTION Continue playing instrumental music. Ask the participants to reflect on the experience they have just gone through by pondering some of the following questions or questions similar to these. You might want to suggest that they respond to the questions that speak most to them. Allow time for them to write their reflections.

- What were my first thoughts or feelings when I entered the nursery?
- How did I complete the room? Did I have a particular theme in mind? If so, what was it?
- What stuffed animals did I notice? Did any have a particular significance for me?

- Who were the loving and nurturing women in my life that came to mind? What did I gain from their loving?
- Who were the women that I witnessed as being loving and nurturing toward others? What did I wish that I had received from these women?
- What is the good quality portrayed by my mother or someone I consider a mother? Do I live out this quality? Why or why not?
- What was my emotional reaction when Mary came to visit me in the nursery? Where did this feeling come from?
- What did Mary comment about the room I completed?
- Was it difficult to tell Mary about the empty spaces in my life that need mothering? What did I tell her?
- Did I believe Mary when she told me that God loves me more than the tenderest woman of my memory? Why or why not?
- What did I name as moments of God's mothering in my life or in someone else's life?
- Could I allow myself to feel God's warmth and mothering? If so, what did it feel like? If not, what did that feel like?
- Did any of God's words touch me with more meaning than others? Comment.
- What was it like for me to image myself in the womb of God? Comment.
- Can I now grasp more deeply the image of God as mother? Explain.
- What is the most special message or image that I will remember from this prayer experience?

Invite and encourage the participants to share their reflections, but do this without pressuring them to open up. Explain that sharing faith experiences can deepen and strengthen one another's faith, and that they need share only what they are comfortable disclosing to the group. Continue playing instrumental music, as it helps with reverencing the moment. Allow time for the sharing and affirming of each person.

ART EXPRESSION AND PRAYER RITUAL (OPTIONAL)

The art expression and prayer ritual is an optional activity. It can be used in place of the reflection questions. If you decide to use one of these activities, prepare the art area before the group gathers.

After the meditation, continue to play quiet music in the art area. Invite the participants to move quietly to one of the prepared places.

Art Expression 1

Set a place for each participant with a 12-by-15-inch scrap of pastel material, a safety or diaper pin, five small sheets of paper, and a pen or pencil.

Instruct the participants to position the "blanket" in front of them like a diamond and to fold it as though there were a baby inside. Invite them to write their reflections on each of the following topics on a separate sheet of paper:

- the women who loved and nurtured them
- the women whom they witnessed as being loving and nurturing toward others
- the good quality that their mother or someone like a mother portrayed
- times when they experienced a mothering God in their life
- what they most need right now to mother the empty spaces they might possess

Have the participants place their pieces of paper within the baby blanket.

Art Expression 2

Set a place for each participant with white art paper and crayons or markers.

Instruct the participants to depict one part of the scene in the nursery. Perhaps they could draw a stuffed animal, show the color of the nursery, or use a color to represent how it felt to be with Mary in the presence of a mothering God. Encourage them to draw or symbolize something special that they want to remember from their prayer experience.

Art Expression 3   Set a place for each participant with colored construction paper, glue, markers or crayons, and scissors.

Instruct the participants to make a Mother's Day card for God. Invite them to be as creative as they want.

After any of the art projects, explain to the participants that by sharing our faith experiences, we can help strengthen one another's faith. Then invite them to share the effect that the prayer time had on them by explaining the significance of the colors and any other symbolism in their artwork. Add that after they have finished describing their artwork, they are to raise it high as a sign of offering themselves back to the God who birthed them. Perhaps they could pray, "Mother God, I believe I am born of your womb and heart. Thank you," or something similar as they lift up their art expression and place it in a cradle or some other designated spot.

Allow time for the sharing and affirming of each person. Continue playing instrumental music, as it helps with reverencing the moment. Remind the participants that they can return to their imagination at any time and be in the presence of their Mother God and call on Mary if they need help. Encourage them to place their art expression in a visible spot in their home as a reminder of the tenderness and faithfulness with which God holds them.

CLOSING   For closure to the meditation experience, slowly and quietly read aloud the following prayer:

> Mother God, may we who have been created in your very womb and loved from your very heart, always come to you for the nurturing we need as your children. Give us the grace to draw nourishment from you so that we might reach out with greater tenderness to those around us. Help us to be gentle with ourselves when we are experiencing a loss of mothering, and to realize that all we need is to seek you, O God of all

mothering. . . . Yes, to seek you, who cuddles us and promises to every one of us, "I will never forget you." Empower us this day and always with your gracious mothering. Amen.

Potter
Shaped and Reshaped

This affirming prayer experience, "Shaped and Reshaped," is based on Jeremiah's image of God as potter. It reminds us to surrender like Jeremiah did and to become supple clay in the Potter's hands so that we might be molded into something new and beautiful and of good service. It is what our great God intended from the beginning of time.

THEME   After you have given directions to the participants and set the tone for meditation, introduce the theme by saying something like the following:

> Jeremiah offers us a gift in giving us the image of God as potter and of us as clay. It is no small thing to be held with an artist's reverence, anticipation, and enthusiasm, as the idea for something great and significant takes form and is shaped and reshaped, and then gloriously realized. We will be able to truly see how our God sees us if we allow ourselves to be clay in the hands of the Master Potter in the privacy of our quiet place apart.

OPENING   Read aloud this opening prayer:

> Potter God, you are the artist who so reverently holds us as clay in your hands. Help us to relinquish any resistance, as we allow ourselves to become vulnerable to your design. Grace us with quiet so that we might truly be able to see ourselves as you see us, shaped and reshaped into the unique and wonderful someone that you intended. We ask this with confidence. Amen.

SCRIPTURE   Read aloud Jeremiah 18:1–6, using a Bible.

SCRIPT Play the "Shaped and Reshaped" meditation on the accompanying recording, or slowly and reverently read aloud the following script for the guided meditation. Play soft, instrumental background music.

Today you will enter the hush of your quiet place and meet Jesus in your imagination. First, you will begin by doing some deep-breathing exercises. When I say to, if you can, breathe in and out through your nose very quietly during these exercises. Close your eyes and get comfortable. You will be relaxing your entire body.

Breathe in deeply . . . hold it . . . breathe out slowly and completely. Breathe in deeply . . . hold it . . . breathe out slowly and completely. Again, breathe in deeply . . . hold it . . . breathe out slowly and completely.

Allow your feet and ankles to relax. . . . Relax your legs . . . and your hips. . . . Stay mindful of your breathing. Relax your stomach muscles . . . and now your chest. . . . Just relax. . . . Let your arms grow limp. . . . Relax your wrists, . . . your hands, . . . and your fingers. . . . Keep breathing in deeply and out slowly.

Allow your shoulders to become heavy. . . . Let all the tension drain from your shoulders. . . . Relax your neck, . . . your facial muscles, . . . your forehead, . . . and even your eyelids. . . . Just relax. . . . Breathe in deeply . . . hold it . . . breathe out slowly and completely. [Pause.]

You are safely walking a path by yourself in the woods. Sunlight plays through the branches and kisses tips of leaves and blades of grass. It is very peaceful here. As you continue to walk the path, you notice a shed around the next bend. It looks rather rustic, yet inviting. There is no door, only an open archway, which makes it even more welcoming. A sign over the door says, "The Potter's." Go ahead in. . . . All around the walls are shelves filled with pottery. Some are whole and beautiful in their design. Others are incomplete, cracked, chipped, or broken altogether. Yet, you notice none of them has been thrown away.

In the middle of the room is a workbench with a piece of freshly cloth-wrapped clay. On the floor is a potter's wheel with a bowl of water beside it. As you step closer to the work table, notice the note resting beside the clay. It has your name on it. Unfold the note and read these words: "Welcome, Friend! . . . This clay is for you. . . . Mold and fashion it into a symbol that represents yourself. . . . Don't be anxious . . . just relax and enjoy it."

Pick up the clay and unwrap it. . . . Think for a moment about how you might mold your clay. . . . Perhaps your shaping of the clay will pertain to where you've been . . . or where you are . . . or where you're going in life. . . . Just let it symbolize how you see yourself. Dip your hands in the cool water and begin working the clay. . . . You can choose to use the potter's wheel or not. . . . Just take this time to continue molding it until you have fashioned it into an image of yourself that you can relate to and that seems right. [Pause.]

Just as you are about finished, a shadow falls across the doorway which causes you to look up. . . . In walks Jesus . . . the Master Potter! . . . He greets you by name, . . . walks over toward you, . . . smiles at the artwork in your hands, and gently takes it in his own. Watch him, while with tender care, he reshapes it into something new. [Pause.]

Reverently, Jesus places the clay image back into your hands. . . . He looks at you with love and says, "This is how I see you. . . ." Listen as he explains the image that he has shaped, . . . and notice what you are feeling as you hear Jesus tell you what he has fashioned and why. [Pause.]

Take some time now to respond to Jesus. Share with him if it is difficult or easy to see yourself as he sees you. . . . Tell him why. . . . Tell him anything in your heart that you would like to refashion with his help. [Pause.]

Jesus has something he wishes to say to you. . . . What is it? Listen closely. [Pause.]

He places both his warm, gentle hands around yours, which are still holding the clay image. He bows his head. You bow yours. He prays for you with love. [Pause.]

When he lifts his head, he is smiling at you. He tells you that it is time for him to go. Say your good-bye to Jesus in a way that is both comfortable and expressive of your present emotions. [Pause.]

Go to the open archway and watch Jesus disappear into the woods. Notice what you are feeling because of his departure.

Return to the stool and reflect on this quiet time you have enjoyed with Jesus. . . . Look at the clay image shaped and reshaped to truly represent you. . . . It is the moment to remember and say to yourself, "He is the potter, and I am the clay. . . ."

Breathe in deeply . . . hold it . . . breathe out slowly and completely. Breathe in deeply . . . hold it . . . breathe out slowly and completely.

Once more, breathe in deeply . . . hold it . . . breathe out slowly and completely. And when you are ready, you may open your eyes.

REFLECTION Continue to play instrumental music. Ask the participants to reflect on the experience they have just gone through by pondering some of the following questions or questions similar to these. You might want to suggest that they respond to the questions that speak most to them. Allow time for them to write their reflections.

- What did I first think when I entered the potter's shed?
- Did any piece of pottery on the shelf speak to me? If so, how?
- How did I react when I saw that the note was for me?
- What did I feel when I knew I had to mold the clay into some symbol or image of how I saw myself?
- What was my experience as I worked the clay? Was it easy or difficult? Explain.
- What did I fashion?
- How did I feel when Jesus entered the shack?
- Did I have any particular reaction when Jesus looked at my clay piece?
- How did it feel to see Jesus begin to rework the clay? Where did those feelings come from?
- What was the image Jesus created of me? Was it totally different from mine? somewhat similar? Comment.
- What will I remember from Jesus' explanation of his symbol for me?
- What will I remember from his prayer for me?
- What did I hope to refashion in my life with Jesus' help? Did I tell him that?
- Could I allow myself to feel the warmth of his hands as they surrounded mine holding the clay piece? How did it feel to be touched by Jesus?
- Am I in a better place because of this prayer time? Comment.
- What emotion(s) did I feel when Jesus had to go?

- How did we express our good-byes?
- Do I believe that I will willingly surrender to the Master Potter by becoming more supple like clay?
- What is the most special image or message that I will remember from this prayer experience?

Invite and encourage the participants to share their reflections, but do this without pressuring them to open up. Explain that sharing faith experiences can deepen and strengthen one another's faith, and that they need share only what they are comfortable disclosing to the group. Continue playing instrumental music, as it helps with reverencing the moment. Allow time for the sharing and affirming of each person.

ART EXPRESSION AND PRAYER RITUAL (OPTIONAL)

The art expression and prayer ritual is an optional activity. It can be used in place of the reflection questions. If you decide to use one of these activities, prepare the art area before the group gathers.

After the meditation, continue playing quiet music in the art area. Invite the participants to move to one of the prepared places.

Art Expression 1

Set a place for each participant with clay, paper towels, and bowls of water (if the type of clay you are using requires water).

Instruct the participants to mold the clay into Jesus' image of them.

After they are finished, allow time for sharing, inviting each participant to tell about Jesus' image of them that they molded out of clay.

Art Expression 2

Set a place for each participant with a sheet of art paper and crayons or markers.

Instruct the participants to draw on one-half of the art paper the clay image they formed to represent themselves, and on the other half to draw the clay image that Jesus fashioned to represent how he saw them. Mention that they can add anything of significance to their artwork to help them remember their prayer experience with Jesus.

After either art expression, explain to the participants that by sharing our faith experiences, we can help strengthen one another's faith. Then invite them to share the effect the prayer time had on them by explaining their clay model or the symbolism in their drawing. Add that after they have finished describing their artwork, perhaps they can lift their artwork high and say, "Lord, help me to remember you are the potter and I am the clay," or something similar before placing their artwork in the middle of the prayer circle or another designated area.

Allow time for the sharing and affirming of each person. Continue playing instrumental music, as it helps with reverencing the moment. Remind the participants that they can return to their imagination at any time and be with Jesus in the potter's shack. Encourage them to place their art expression in a visible spot in their home to remind them of their being shaped and reshaped into something new and wonderful.

CLOSING   For closure to the meditation experience, lead the following prayer of petition:

> *Litany response*
> God, you are the potter, and we are the clay.
>
> *Leader*
> When we want to control situations or people, help us to remember . . . [All respond.]
>
> *Leader*
> When we think we can go it alone, help us to remember . . . [All respond.]

Leader
When we are excited and our pride wants to acknowledge that we have made progress, help us to remember . . . [All respond.]

Leader
When we offer our prayer for the day, help us to remember . . . [All respond.]

Leader
When we dare to hope in our future and in our goals . . . [All respond.]

Leader
When we despair, help us to remember . . . [All respond.]

Leader
When we feel that following your will is too hard, help us to remember . . . [All respond.]

Leader
When we're not sure what we are making of ourselves . . . [All respond.]

Compassion
In the Belly of the Great Fish

This challenging prayer experience, "In the Belly of the Great Fish," is based on the circumstances in the biblical story that led Jonah to be swallowed. Due to his intolerance of others, Jonah failed to do God's will. It reminds us that we too are in the belly of the great fish when we allow ourselves to be motivated by unkindness and prejudice. It is only by praying for our own deliverance and following God's will that we are saved.

THEME   After you have given directions to the participants and set the tone for meditation, introduce the theme by saying something like the following:

> Our God possesses and offers a universal love. Because we are made in God's image, it is only right that we ourselves develop and practice a universal love too. In the story about Jonah, we witness his being swallowed up in the belly of a great fish, his praying for deliverance, and his eventual willingness to do God's will to save the enemy. In this metaphorical tale, Jonah finally learns what kind of unrestrained love God offers. Like Jonah, it is just as important for us to examine that which keeps us from genuinely reaching out with a universal love.

OPENING   Read aloud this opening prayer:

> Universal God, your love and forgiveness are unsurpassed. Be with us today so that we might honestly examine our prejudices, our unkind motives, and the restraints we put on our own loving of others. Grant us

the grace to practice caring and forgiving in the same unmeasured way that you do. Meet us now in the stillness of our quiet place apart so that you may deliver us from the darkness of the great fish's belly, and so that we may begin to love with a universality. We ask this of you, trusting in your power to free us from our destructive intolerance of others. Amen.

SCRIPTURE   Read aloud the Book of Jonah, using a Bible.

SCRIPT   Play the "In the Belly of the Great Fish" meditation on the accompanying recording, or slowly and reverently read aloud the following script for the guided meditation. Play soft, instrumental background music.

Today you will enter the hush of your quiet place and meet Jesus in your imagination.

First, you will begin by doing some deep-breathing exercises. When I say to, if you can, breathe in and out through your nose very quietly during these exercises. Close your eyes and get comfortable. You will be relaxing your entire body.

Breathe in deeply . . . hold it . . . breathe out slowly and completely. Breathe in deeply . . . hold it . . . breathe out slowly and completely. Again, breathe in deeply . . . hold it . . . breathe out slowly and completely.

Allow your feet and ankles to relax. . . . Relax your legs . . . and your hips. . . . Stay mindful of your breathing. Relax your stomach muscles . . . and now your chest. . . . Just relax. . . . Let your arms grow limp. . . . Relax your wrists, . . . your hands, . . . and your fingers. . . . Keep breathing in deeply and out slowly.

Allow your shoulders to become heavy. . . . Let all the tension drain from your shoulders. . . .

Relax your neck, . . . your facial muscles, . . .
your forehead, . . . and even your eyelids. . . .
Just relax. . . . Breathe in deeply . . . hold it . . .
breathe out slowly and completely. [Pause.]

Today, you are quietly walking on the docks by
the sea. Seagulls screech overhead, the waves pound
out a musical in their surf, and fishing boats lap
against their moorings. . . . Listen to the sounds
around you. . . . You are alone. Breathe in the
fresh salt air. . . . At the end of the dock, you
notice a shack with a bench out in front. It seems a
welcoming place to sit and think. As you get closer
to the bench, you notice a colorful painting hanging on the wall just above it. . . . Curious . . .
you go forward to look at it. . . . It is an oil painting of Jonah being spewed from the belly of a
whale. . . . Jonah, whose "I'm better than you"
attitude got him into trouble in the first place.

Sit down on the bench and think for a minute
about the moments in which you possess an "I'm
better than you" attitude. . . . To whom do you
flaunt this? . . . Who are the persons or types of
persons that you consider less important than you?
. . . Toward whom do you direct your prejudice?
. . . Whom wouldn't you bother to help because
they are different from you? . . . Take this time to
examine your conscience. [Pause.]

The sound of footsteps causes you to look up.
. . . Jesus approaches you. . . . Notice how you
are feeling to have Jesus come to you during this
examination of your prejudices. . . .

But, as Jesus greets you by name and sits beside
you, . . . he is smiling at you. . . . Listen as he
tells you, "Jonah firmly believed in God's power to
free him from the belly of the great fish, . . . and

so he confidently prayed for his own deliverance.
. . ."

He now tells you, "For you to be freed from
the belly of your own great fish, you must now
share with me the ways in which you have been
openly intolerant of others. . . ." Take this time
to name people and ways in which you have been
unkind and prejudicial toward others. . . . Name
anyone that you look down upon and believe isn't
as good as you or isn't a worthwhile person. Name
anyone whom you refrain from loving. [Pause.]

Jesus challenges you to choose someone that
you can reach out to or to decide on an action that
you can do to show your growing acceptance of
others. . . . You think about what you might do.
. . . Tell Jesus now what you are planning to do,
whom you are choosing to reach out to. [Pause.]
Do you feel differently in choosing kindness rather
than intolerance? . . .

Jesus invites you to pray with him with re-
newed confidence in the God who can deliver you,
just as Jonah was delivered. . . . Listen to Jesus
pray for you. . . . What do you add to the prayer?
. . . Bow your head and pray the words of Jonah,
"Compassionate and gracious God, have mercy on
me. . . ."

It is time for Jesus to go. He stands and faces
you with love. It is clear that he has forgiven you
for your prejudices. It is clear that he believes that
you can leave the belly of your own great fish and
reach out to others with caring acceptance. Allow
yourself to receive the safe and gentle hug that Jesus
has for you. . . . Listen as he whispers, "Love
others as you love yourself. . . . Remember, it is
how I love you. . . ."

Watch as Jesus walks the length of the dock and disappears from sight. . . . Return to the bench and sit quietly, listening to the gulls and the waves, and remembering that you are called to love with a universal love. . . . As you sit for a moment, feel God's love surround and embrace you unconditionally. . . . Just breathe in God's unrestrained love for you. . . . Vow to carry out your loving acceptance of others. . . .

Breathe in deeply . . . hold it . . . breathe out slowly and completely. Breathe in deeply . . . hold it . . . breathe out slowly and completely. Once more, breathe in deeply . . . hold it . . . breathe out slowly and completely. And when you are ready, you may open your eyes.

REFLECTION Continue to play instrumental music. Ask the participants to reflect on the experience they have just gone through by pondering some of the following questions or questions similar to these. You might want to suggest that they respond to the questions that speak most to them. Allow time for them to write their reflections.

- How did it feel to be quietly alone and walking the docks by the sea?
- What was my reaction to seeing the painting of Jonah being spewed from the great fish's mouth?
- To whom have I displayed an "I'm better than you" attitude? Why?
- Who are persons or types of persons that I consider less important than me? Why do I consider them less important?
- Who bears the brunt of my prejudices?
- Whom have I refused to help because of their differences? How did I feel when I refused to help?
- What did I feel when Jesus came upon me during the examination of my prejudices?

- Whom did I name for Jesus as having received my open intolerance? Whom have I refrained from loving? Did I share everything? everyone?
- Whom did I name as the person I will reach out to in order to show my growing acceptance of others? Or what action did I promise Jesus that I would take?
- How and what do I feel when I choose kindness over intolerance?
- What is the prayer Jesus prays for me? What do I add to the prayer?
- Do I believe God will deliver me from the belly of my own great fish?
- Do I sense Jesus' forgiveness of my prejudices?
- Could I allow Jesus to hug me? Did I feel loved at that moment? Explain.
- Will I try more sincerely to love with a universal love? How will I do this?
- What is the most special message or image that I will remember from this prayer experience?

Invite and encourage the participants to share their reflections, but do this without pressuring them to open up. Explain that sharing faith experiences can deepen and strengthen one another's faith, and that they need share only what they are comfortable disclosing to the group. Continue playing instrumental music, as it helps with reverencing the moment. Allow time for the sharing and affirming of each person.

ART EXPRESSION AND PRAYER RITUAL (OPTIONAL)

The art expression and prayer ritual is an optional activity. It can be used in place of the reflection questions. If you decide to use one of these activities, prepare the art area before the group gathers.

After the meditation, continue playing quiet music in the art area. Invite the participants to move to one of the prepared places.

Art Expression 1   Set each place with a sheet of art paper and markers or crayons.

Direct the participants to draw a whale, and within its belly, to write or depict with symbols or colors the prejudices and intolerance they have shown others. All around the outside of the whale, invite them to write or depict with symbols or colors the new action they will take to love with a universal love.

Art Expression 2   Set a place for each participant with art paper, watercolor paints, a paintbrush, a small container of water, and paper towels.

Instruct the participants to paint a scene from their meditation, and to indicate through colors, symbols, or words what their time with Jesus meant to them.

After either art expression, explain to the participants that by sharing our faith experiences, we can help strengthen one another's faith. Then invite them to share the effect the prayer time had on them by explaining the colors and symbolism of their artwork. Add that after they have finished describing their art expression, they are to place it in the middle of the prayer circle or another designated place. Perhaps they could pray, "Compassionate and gracious God of Jonah, have mercy on me," or something similar as they set their artwork down.

Allow time for the sharing and affirming of each person. Continue playing instrumental music, as it helps with reverencing the moment. Remind the participants that they can return to their imagination at any time and be with Jesus in this very real way. Suggest that they place their artwork in a visible spot in their home to remind them that they must strive to love with a universal love.

CLOSING   For closure to the meditation experience, lead the following litany of petition:

Litany response
O, compassionate and gracious God of Jonah, have mercy on us.

Leader
For the times when we have shunned someone of a different socioeconomic class . . . [All respond.]

Leader
For the times we have overtly belittled others and refused to care or act in justice . . . [All respond.]

Leader
For all thoughts and situations in which we have discriminated against another child of God due to race, religion, or sexual orientation . . . [All respond.]

Leader
For the moments when we acted with an "I'm better than you" attitude . . . [All respond.]

Leader
For our failure to reverence the homeless, the aged, the poor, the war veteran, the welfare recipient . . . [All respond.]

Leader
For our lack of acceptance of any marginalized and alienated human person . . . [All respond.]

Leader
For our apathy toward any individual or group of people who needed our help . . . [All respond.]

Invite the participants to add any other prayer intentions. When all have finished, close by praying once more, "O compassionate and gracious God of Jonah, have mercy on us."

Love
Reflection in the Mirror

This enlightening prayer experience, "Reflection in the Mirror," is based on the passage from Saint Paul's First Letter to the Corinthians, in which he extols the virtue of love. It is love that brings us toward perfection. And to mirror love is to make manifest the image of God.

THEME   After you have given directions to the participants and set the tone for meditation, introduce the theme by saying something like the following:

> God is love. That is what Jesus said. We are called to love and so be an image of the God who is love. It is essential that we pause to reflect on our failures at love so that we might grow in our loving. Holding the mirror up to ourselves is to examine how we do and don't reflect God, who is the culmination of the virtue of love that Saint Paul talks about. We can challenge ourselves to the truth if we but risk and enter our quiet place apart.

OPENING   Read aloud this opening prayer:

> God, who is love, make yourself known to us this day so that we might appreciate you as you truly are, and learn to recognize you in the reflection of ourselves. Allow our hearts to be open, to seek the honesty with which we must examine ourselves so that in the end, we may be as the reflection of you in a mirror—pure love. We ask this of you with trust in your direction and compassion. Amen.

SCRIPTURE Read aloud 1 Corinthians, chapter 13, using a Bible.

SCRIPT Play the "Reflection in the Mirror" meditation on the accompanying recording, or slowly and reverently read aloud the following script for the guided meditation. Play soft, instrumental background music.

Today you will enter the hush of your quiet place and meet Jesus in your imagination. First, you will begin by doing some deep-breathing exercises. When I say to, if you can, breathe in and out through your nose very quietly during these exercises. Close your eyes and get comfortable. You will be relaxing your entire body.

Breathe in deeply . . . hold it . . . breathe out slowly and completely. Breathe in deeply . . . hold it . . . breathe out slowly and completely. Again, breathe in deeply . . . hold it . . . breathe out slowly and completely.

Allow your feet and ankles to relax. . . . Relax your legs . . . and your hips. . . . Stay mindful of your breathing. Relax your stomach muscles . . . and now your chest. . . . Just relax. . . . Let your arms grow limp. . . . Relax your wrists, . . . your hands, . . . and your fingers. . . . Keep breathing in deeply and out slowly.

Allow your shoulders to become heavy. . . . Let all the tension drain from your shoulders. . . . Relax your neck, . . . your facial muscles, . . . your forehead, . . . and even your eyelids. . . . Just relax. . . . Breathe in deeply . . . hold it . . . breathe out slowly and completely. [Pause.]

You are restfully curled up on a comfortable couch thinking about yourself and your ability to love. . . . Think of the most loving thing that you have done or said lately. . . .

There is a quiet knock at the door; you have a visitor. . . . Your guest is Jesus. . . . It is with joy that he softly greets you by name . . . and tells you that he is glad to have time with you. . . . Offer Jesus a spot on the couch where he can settle comfortably also. As you look over at him, he seems quite at ease. . . . Notice what you are feeling to have Jesus join you. . . .

Intently, Jesus leans toward you and tells you that in Saint Paul's letter, the disciple is speaking of God as he wrote of the virtue of love. . . . He tells you that he wants you to understand this. . . . Jesus has brought a large hand mirror with him and holds it up to his face as he shares the Scripture passage with you in a new way. Listen closely; instead of the word *love,* Jesus uses *God.* Watch Jesus' face in the mirror as he speaks. "God is patient. . . . God is kind. . . . God is not envious. . . . God does not boast. . . . God is not proud. . . . God is not rude. . . . God is not self-seeking. . . . God is not easily angered. . . . God keeps no record of wrongs. . . . God does not delight in evil, but rejoices with the truth. . . . God always protects, always trusts, always hopes, always perseveres. . . . God never fails. . . ." Jesus' eyes sparkle back at you from his reflection in the mirror. Allow yourself to experience the awareness that you are in the presence of your God, who is love. . . .

Jesus turns toward you and tells you, when you are your best self, you are a reflection of God . . . a reflection of love. Jesus holds up the mirror now for you to see yourself. Try not to feel uncomfortable, but listen as Jesus repeats the passage using your name each time. . . . And with each sentence, think of a moment in which you lived out the virtue being named. You, _____, are patient. . . . You, _____, are kind. . . . You, _____, are not envious. . . . You, _____, do not boast. . . . You, _____, are not proud. . . . You, _____, are not rude. . . . You, _____, are not self-seeking. . . . You, _____, are not easily angered. . . . You, _____, keep no record of wrongs. . . . You, _____, do not delight in evil, but rejoice with the truth. . . . You, _____, protect. . . . You, _____, trust. . . . You, _____, hope. . . . You, _____, persevere. . . . You, _____, never fail. . . .

Quietly, take all this in. . . . When you are your best self, you are a reflection of God, who is love. Allow yourself to smile with this image. . . . With his head close to yours in the mirror, Jesus thanks you for those times when you have been a reflection of God. . . .

Gently, Jesus puts the mirror down and asks you to now share how and when you have not mirrored God's love. . . . Tell Jesus your shortcomings, and anything and everything you have done which has not been loving, so that you might secure his help and guidance. [Pause.]

Take care to listen to the response he gives you. [Pause.]

Jesus tenderly places one hand upon your shoulder and the other on your head in blessing. . . . Allow yourself to feel the strength and empowerment Jesus offers you in this gesture. . . . Bow your head and hear the prayer Jesus has for you. [Pause.] Notice what you are feeling at this moment.

It is time for Jesus to leave you. Say your good-byes in whatever way expresses what you are feeling and thinking. [Pause.]

With one last look of love and encouragement, Jesus leaves you. . . .

Settle back comfortably on the couch and allow yourself these few moments to grow stronger in your resolve to be a reflection of God's love. . . .

Breathe in deeply . . . hold it . . . breathe out slowly and completely. Breathe in deeply . . . hold it . . . breathe out slowly and completely. Once more, breathe in deeply . . . hold it . . . breathe out slowly and completely. And when you are ready, you may open your eyes.

REFLECTION Continue playing instrumental music. Ask the participants to reflect on the experience they have just gone through by pondering some of the following questions or questions similar to these. You might want to suggest that they respond to the questions that speak most to them. Allow time for them to write their reflections.

- How was it for me to be comfortably curled up on the couch and have Jesus visit me?
- Did it make sense to me that Jesus changed the word *love* to *God* in the scriptural passage? What was it like for me to look at Jesus in the mirror when he spoke?
- What was I thinking and feeling when Jesus placed my name in the passage? What emotions did I feel when Jesus held the mirror up to me? Comment.
- Could I agree that as my best self, I am a reflection of God? of love?
- What shortcomings did I need to share with Jesus so that I might receive help and guidance?
- What did Jesus say in response to what I told him?
- Could I feel the strength and empowerment Jesus offered through his warm touch on my head and shoulder? What did that feel like?

- What was Jesus' prayer for me? How did I feel to hear it?
- How did we express our good-byes to each other? What was said?
- Do I believe that I am more resolved to reflect God, who is love? Comment.
- What is the most special message or image that I will remember from this prayer experience?

Invite and encourage the participants to share their reflections, but do this without pressuring them to open up. Explain that sharing faith experiences can deepen and strengthen one another's faith, and that they need share only what they are comfortable disclosing to the group. Continue playing instrumental music, as it helps with reverencing the moment. Allow time for the sharing and affirming of each person.

ART EXPRESSION AND PRAYER RITUAL (OPTIONAL)

The art expression and prayer ritual is an optional activity. It can be used in place of the reflection questions. If you decide to use one of these activities, prepare the art area before the group gathers.

After the meditation, continue to play quiet music in the art area. Invite the participants to move to one of the prepared places.

Art Expression 1

Set a place for each participant with white art paper, various shades of construction paper, markers or pens, and glue.

Direct the participants to tear small shapes out of the construction paper and to make two collages on their art paper. On one half of the paper, instruct them to make a collage of colors to represent them at their best selves, when they are truly a reflection of God, who is love. On the other half, tell them to make a collage of colors representing themselves when they are lacking in their love and have become less than mirror images in their reflection of who God is.

Art Expression 2 Set a place for each participant with a 5-by-8-inch piece of wood for a plaque, a small craft mirror (or piece of foil), markers or crayons, scissors, glue, the Scripture passage from First Corinthians, various shades of construction paper, and a bracket to nail on the back of their artwork for hanging. Have hammers and a finishing spray such as polyurethane available.

Instruct the participants first to cut a strip of paper on which they are to write their name and the verb *is*. (For example, Jane is . . .) Then tell them to cut various shapes and sizes of construction paper and to write on them the virtues from the Scripture passage that best describe themselves when they truly reflect the God who is love. Direct the participants to glue their mirror (or foil piece) on their wood and to decoratively place and glue on the wood their name and the virtues they have chosen. If necessary, cover the mirror or foil piece before spraying the artwork with the finishing spray.

After either art expression, explain to the participants that by sharing our faith experiences, we can help strengthen one another's faith. Then invite them to share the effect the prayer time had on them by explaining the significance of the colors, words, or symbols expressed in their artwork. Add that after they have finished describing their artwork, they are to reverently lift it high and then place it in the middle of the prayer circle or another designated spot. Perhaps they could pray, "God, who is love, may I always mirror a reflection of you," or something similar as they do so.

Allow time for the sharing and affirming of each person. Continue playing instrumental music, as it helps with reverencing the moment. Remind the participants that they can return to their imagination at any time and be in the presence of our God, who is love, in this very real way. Encourage them to place their art expression in a visible spot in their home as a reminder of their time spent with Jesus.

CLOSING   For closure to the meditation experience, have different participants share in reading aloud the following prayer of petition:

> *Litany response*
> God, who is love, may we come to be a reflection of you.
>
> *Leader*
> During times when patience and kindness elude us . . . [All respond.]
>
> *Leader*
> When envious, rude, or angry emotions want to control us . . . [All respond.]
>
> *Leader*
> For those situations in which we want our needs to come before the needs of others . . . [All respond.]
>
> *Leader*
> During moments when we are tempted to boast and allow selfish pride to surface . . . [All respond.]
>
> *Leader*
> At any time when we fail to trust and persevere . . . [All respond.]
>
> *Leader*
> When we lose hope and falter because we feel unloved or unworthy . . . [All respond.]
>
> *Leader*
> When we get in our own way and feel smug because someone "got what was coming to them" . . . [All respond.]

Leader
When we lack in expressing your love, which we should
be mirroring at all times . . . [All respond.]

Leader
When we hold a grudge and want to gossip about
someone who has hurt us . . . [All respond.]

Leader
When someone has done good for another, help us to
rejoice and say . . . [All respond.]

ACKNOWLEDGMENTS
(continued)

Sincere and loving appreciation to Barry Russo for once again sharing his musical talent that gently invites us to prayer.

To Anthony "Barrel" Marrapese of Reel to Real Recording Studio, Cranston, Rhode Island, I express deep gratitude for his expertise in his profession but also for sharing his faith and his very self in our sessions.

For the humorous conversation and support I receive from my editor, Carl Koch, I am genuinely grateful.

And to all those who have shared an image of their God that aided me in my own: Aggie, Isabel, Shirley, Pauline, Jean, Eileen, Father Jude, Sister Mary George, the Doyles, retreatants, conference attendees, catechists, children, parishioners, and all those in my own incredible large and faith-filled family. I thank you and wish your image of the Holy One to never stop expanding.

Other titles in the A Quiet Place Apart series available from Saint Mary's Press

Each of the titles in this series has a leader's guide and recordings of the meditation scripts. The leader's guide contains directions for preparing the meditations, the meditation scripts, and suggestions for follow-up after the meditations. The audiocassette and the compact disc contain high-quality recordings of the meditation scripts against a background of original music.

Guided Meditations for Adults:
Salvation, Joy, Faith, Healing

Guided Meditations for Youth
on Personal Themes

Guided Meditations for Youth
on Sacramental Life

Guided Meditations for Junior High:
Good Judgment, Gifts, Obedience, Inner Blindness

Guided Meditations for Advent,
Christmas, New Year, and Epiphany

Guided Meditations for Lent, Holy Week,
Easter, and Pentecost

Guided Meditations for Ordinary Time:
Courage, Loss, Gratitude, and Needs

Order from your local religious bookstore or from

Saint Mary's Press
702 TERRACE HEIGHTS
WINONA, MN 55987-1320
1-800-533-8095